Copyright © 2015 by Lisa R. Cohen

All rights reserved. This book or any portion thereof may not be reproduced or used in any manner whatsoever without the express written permission of the publisher except for the use of brief quotations in a book review

Amazon.com/ author/ Lisa R. Cohen

ISBN-13: 978-1523279586

ISBN-10: 1523279583

Cheesy Chocolaty Donut Balls	4
Delightful Nutty Bacon Donuts	6
Cinnamon Flavored Donuts with Orange Syrup	8
Cherry Magic Donuts	10
Chocolate & Zucchini Donut Delight	12
Chocolate and Spinach Health Enhancer	14
Peanut Donuts with Orange Topping	16
Almond Blast Donuts with Lemon Topping	18
Bacon Magical Donut with Cinnamon Syrup	20
Simple and Tasty Spicy Donuts	22
Jam Filled Strawberry Donuts	24
Creamy and Cheesy Donuts	26
Orange Filled Donut Magic	28
Cheesy Apple and Cinnamon Blast	30
Fruity and Nutty Magical Donuts	32
Coconut Magic Donuts	34
Healthy and Tasty Pumpkin Blast	36
Cheese Coated Chocolaty Donuts:	38
Blueberry Delightful Donuts with orange Coating	41
Simple Cream Glazed Donuts	43
Healthy and Spicy Spinach Donuts	45
Easy to make Strawberry Donuts	47
Double Orange Blast Donuts	49
Almond Punch Donuts	51
Choco-Nutty Fantastic Donut	53
Vanilla and Chocolate Smashing Donuts	55
Simplest Chocolate Donuts	57
Mom's Magic Strawberry Donuts	59
Banana & Coconut Protein Punch	61
Protein Boosting Strawberry Donuts	63

Pumpkin Pie Flavorful Donuts	65
Magical Spicy Zucchini Donuts	67
Apple-Maple Mysterious Donut	69
Raspberry Sweet Fantasy Donut	71
Nut Blast Donuts with Cheese Topping	73

Cheesy Chocolaty Donut Balls

Total time: 40 mins

Servings: 6

Ingredients:

    1 packet splenda

    3 eggs, separated

    1/8 tsp cream of tartar

    1 tsp baking powder

    3 oz cream cheese

    2 tbsp sugar free vanilla syrup

    1 tbsp sugar free vanilla syrup

    1 oz dark chocolate

    2 tbsp heavy whipping cream

    2 tbsp butter

    2 packets of splenda (small)

Directions:

Blend the cream of tartar with the egg whites till the mixture forms stiff peaks. Now mix the egg yolks with the cream cheese along with splenda, vanilla and baking powder. Incorporate the egg white mixture to this mixture and pour the batter into cupcake shells. Bake them in a preheated oven for 30 minutes at 300 degrees.

Now make the chocolate sauce by cooking all the ingredients in microwave oven and simply pour the mixture over the donuts.

Nutrition per Serving

Protein: 8g

Fat: 24g

Carbohydrate: 3g Net

Delightful Nutty Bacon Donuts

Total time: 12 mins

Servings: 6

Ingredients:

½ cup cooked and crumbled pork (drain off excess fat)

3 tbsp erythritol

½ tsp maple flavouring

½ tsp vanilla extract

1 egg

Olive oil

¼ tsp baking powder

1 tbsp almonds, chopped

Directions:

Put the bacon crumbles in a food processor along with the almonds and pulse them for a few seconds.

Pour in the egg along with all other ingredients and pulse to make smooth batter.

Coat the donut maker with olive oil and pour the batter into the wells. Cook for 12 minutes (approx.) and serve warm.

Nutrition per Serving

Protein: 3.9g

Fat: 12g

Carbohydrate: 1.7g Net

Cinnamon Flavored Donuts with Orange Syrup

Total time: 15 mins

Servings: 10

Ingredients for donuts:

1/3 cup coconut oil

2 packets of vanilla protein powder

¼ tsp ground cloves

3 tbsp molasses

1 tsp vanilla extract

1 tbsp stevia powder

3 eggs

2 tsp ground cinnamon

¾ cup almond meal

2 tsp ground ginger

1 cup baking blend (gluten free)

½ tsp salt

1/3 tsp baking soda

Ingredients for orange syrup:

2 tsp fresh orange juice

2 tbsp coconut milk

1 tbsp stevia powder

Few drops of orange flavor

1 tbsp vanilla protein powder

2 tbsp orange zest

1 tbsp coconut butter

Directions:

Mix all the donut making ingredients to make the batter and pour into cupcake molds. Cook the donuts in preheated oven for 12 minutes at 350 degrees.

Make the orange syrup by blending all the ingredients together to make the smooth liquid and drizzle the mixture over the cooked donuts. Allow some resting time and then serve.

Nutrition per Serving

Protein: 2.6g

Fat: 13g

Carbohydrate: 8.2g Net

Cherry Magic Donuts

Total time: 23 mins

Servings: 14

Ingredients:

    2 tsp baking powder

    ½ tsp baking soda

    1 tsp ground cinnamon

    ½ tsp sea salt

    ¼ cup ground chia seeds

    ¼ tsp ground ginger

    1.5 cups blanched almond flour

    ¼ cup coconut flour

    ¾ cup erythritol

    1/8 tsp ground cloves

    1 cup dried cherry

    1/8 tsp cherry flavoring

    3 eggs

    ¼ cup buttermilk

    2 tbsp melted butter

½ tsp liquid stevia

1 tsp apple cider vinegar

Directions:

Blend the dry and wet ingredients separately in two bowls and then mix them together to make the batter for donut.

Keep the donut pan ready by coating with oil and then bake the donuts for 12 minutes. Sprinkle some powdered erythritol on top before serving.

Nutrition per Serving

Protein: 2.1g

Fat: 18g

Carbohydrate: 2.9g Net

Chocolate & Zucchini Donut Delight

Total time: 35 mins

Servings: 25 mins

Ingredients:

    8 oz grated zucchini

    1 egg

    1 tsp baking soda

    8 oz peanut butter

    1 cup erythritol

    1 tsp vanilla extract

    4 oz melted butter

    2 tbsp cocoa powder

Directions:

Pour all the ingredients in a bowl and use a hand blender to make smooth batter for the donuts.

Grease a donut pan with some oil and then pour the batter into it. Bake for 30 minutes and serve warm.

Nutrition per Serving

Protein: 3g

Fat: 5g

Carbohydrate: 2g Net

Chocolate and Spinach Health Enhancer

Total time: 30 mins

Servings: 24

Ingredients:

    16 oz fresh spinach puree

    1 tsp vanilla extract

    1 egg

    1 tsp baking soda

    1/8 tsp sea salt

    8 oz peanut butter

    4 oz melted butter

    2 tbsp cocoa powder

    1 cup erythritol

Directions:

Preheat the oven at 350 degrees and grease the donut pan with cooking spray.

Blend all the ingredients in a bowl with an immersion blender and pour the batter into the donut pan. Bake for 30 minutes and then allow some resting time before serving.

Nutrition per Serving

Protein: 3g

Fat: 5g

Carbohydrate: 2g Net

Peanut Donuts with Orange Topping

Total time: 30 mins

Servings: 12

Ingredients for making donut:

   2 cups peanut flour

   3.5 tsp baking powder

   1 tsp sea salt

   1¼ cups almond milk

   1/8 tsp baking soda

   1 tsp stevia glycerite

   1 tsp vanilla extract

   3 eggs

   ½ cup erythritol

Ingredients for making orange topping:

   ¼ cup erythritol

   ½ tsp vanilla extract

   ¼ cup almond milk (vanilla flavoured)

   4 tbsp orange zest

   2 tbsp orange juice

¼ cup melted butter

Directions:

Coat the donut pan with oil and line with parchment paper.

Mix all the donut ingredients in the food processor to make smooth batter.

Pour batter into the prepared pan and bake for 25 minutes at 350 degrees.

Keep the donuts on wire rack to allow complete cooling.

Make the orange topping by mixing all the ingredients in melted butter. Spread the paste over the donuts and allow some resting time so that the topping can set.

Nutrition per Serving

Protein: 12g

Fat: 8.7g

Carbohydrate: 7.9g Net

Almond Blast Donuts with Lemon Topping

Total time: 30 mins

Servings: 12

Ingredients for making donuts:

  2 cups almond flour

  3.5 tsp baking powder

  1 tsp stevia glycerite

  3 eggs

  ½ cup erythritol

  1 tsp sea salt

  1¼ cups almond milk

  1/8 tsp baking soda

  1 tsp vanilla extract

Ingredients for making lemon topping:

  ¼ cup erythritol

  ½ tsp vanilla extract

  ¼ cup almond milk (vanilla flavoured)

  2 tbsp lemon zest

2 tbsp lemon juice

¼ cup melted butter

Directions:

Keep the oven preheated at 350 degrees and coat the donut pan and then line them with parchment paper.

Blend all the donut ingredients in food processor and then pour the batter into the pan. Bake for 25 minutes and allow complete cooling.

Make the lemon topping by blending all the ingredients and then spread the mixture over the donuts. Allow resting time to set the topping firmly.

Nutrition per Serving

Protein: 12g

Fat: 8.7g

Carbohydrate: 7.9g Net

Bacon Magical Donut with Cinnamon Syrup

Total time: 35 mins

Servings: 12

Ingredients for making donuts:

½ cup butter

¼ cup whey protein powder (unflavored)

2 eggs

¼ tsp stevia extract

¼ cup coconut flour

1.5 cups almond flour

1 tsp cinnamon extract

2 tsp baking powder

½ tsp xanthan gum

½ tsp salt

½ cup erythritol

½ cup almond milk

Ingredients for making bacon topping:

¾ tsp cinnamon extract

8 slices of bacon, cooked till crisp and then chopped

¾ cups powdered erythritol

3 tbsp almond milk

Directions:

Reserve the almond milk and then blend all the wet and dry ingredients in two separate bowls. Blend the two mixtures together to make the batter and then add the almond milk to the batter slowly. It will be best to use an immersion blender to make the batter smooth.

Pour the batter into greased and paper lined donut pan and bake them for 18 minutes. Make sure that the edges become golden brown in color.

Make the bacon topping by blending erythritol with almond milk and cinnamon extract. Top each donut with cinnamon glaze and then sprinkle the bacon pieces. Allow 15 minutes resting time to set the bacon and glaze.

Nutrition per Serving

Protein: 7g

Fat: 19g

Carbohydrate: 6g Net

Simple and Tasty Spicy Donuts

Total time: 20 mins

Servings: 12

Ingredients for making donuts:

¼ cup whey protein powder (unflavored)

2 eggs

¼ tsp stevia extract

¼ cup coconut flour

½ cup erythritol

1.5 cups almond flour

½ cup butter

¼ cardamom powder

2 tsp baking powder

½ tsp xanthan gum

½ tsp salt

½ cup almond milk

Directions:

Keep almond milk aside and blend the wet and dry ingredients in separate bowls. Blend them together and then add the almond milk slowly to make smooth batter for the donuts.

Keep the donut pan ready along with the oven by preheating it at 350 degrees. Pour the batter into the pan and bake the donuts for 18 minutes. Allow complete cooling down in wire rack and then serve.

Nutrition per Serving

Protein: 7g

Fat: 19g

Carbohydrate: 6g Net

Jam Filled Strawberry Donuts

Total time: 15 mins

Servings: 12

Ingredients:

    4 tbsp chocolate flavoured almond milk

    1 egg

    ½ cup chocolate flavored whey

    2 tsp baking powder

    ½ cup erythritol

    1/8 tsp sea salt

    Oil for frying

    12 tsp strawberry jam (for filling)

Directions:

Keep the jam aside and mix all other ingredients to make the donut batter. Heat up oil in a frying pan and then cook 12 donuts. Cook on both sides till the donuts are golden brown in color. Allow complete cooling by putting the donuts on wire rack.

Use a sharp knife to cut through the middle and use a teaspoon to put the strawberry jam filling inside the donut.

Nutrition per Serving

Protein: 0.2g

Fat: 2.3g

Carbohydrate: 1g Net

Creamy and Cheesy Donuts

Total time: 15 mins

Servings: 10

Ingredients:

    2/3 cup coconut flour

    ½ tsp sea salt

    ½ cup erythritol

    1 cup sour cream

    4 tbsp heavy cream

    4 tbsp grated mozzarella cheese

    ½ tsp vanilla

    ½ tsp baking powder

    3 large eggs

    ¾ cup melted butter

Directions:

Mix the dry and wet ingredients in separate bowls and blend them together to make the batter. The batter must be a bit thick.

Grease the donut pan and keep the oven ready by heating it at 300 degrees. Pour the batter into the pan and bake for 12 minutes. Allow cooling down and then serve.

Nutrition per Serving

Protein: 2g

Fat: 28g

Carbohydrate: 2g Net

Orange Filled Donut Magic

Total time: 15 mins

Servings: 12

Ingredients:

    4 tbsp orange flavoured almond milk

    1 egg

    ½ cup orange flavored whey

    2 tsp baking powder

    ½ cup erythritol

    1/8 tsp sea salt

    Oil for frying

    12 tsp orange jam (for filling)

Directions:

Mix the ingredients for making donuts and use a hand blender to make the batter smooth.

Heat oil in a frying pan and cook 12 donuts. You will have to cook till the donuts become golden brown form both sides. Put them on wire rack to allow complete cooling.

Use a knife to cut the middle portion of the donuts and insert a spoonful of orange jam.

Serve by sprinkling some powdered erythritol.

Nutrition per Serving

Protein: 0.2g

Fat: 2.3g

Carbohydrate: 1g Net

Cheesy Apple and Cinnamon Blast

Total time: 12 mins

Servings: 6

Ingredients for making donuts:

    2 tbsp vanilla protein powder

    ¼ tsp xanthan gum

    2 tsp baking powder

    ½ tsp nutmeg

    ½ cup coconut flour

    ¼ tsp kosher salt

    1 tsp ground cinnamon

    2 eggs

    ¼ cup granulated erythritol

    1 tbsp melted butter

    ½ cup apple cider vinegar

Ingredients for making cheesy cinnamon coating:

    ¼ cup powdered erythritol

    4 tbsp melted butter

    1½ tsp ground cinnamon

6 tsp cheese spread

Directions:

Use separate bowls to mix the wet and dry ingredients and then blend them together to make the donut dough. The dough must be a bit firm. Make six small balls from the dough and shape them like simple old donuts.

Heat oil and fry the donuts till both sides turn golden brown in color and then allow them to cool down completely.

Make a mixture with melted butter erythritol, cheese spread and cinnamon powder. Spread the mixture over the donuts and let the topping rest for some time.

Nutrition per Serving

Protein: 9g

Fat: 17g

Carbohydrate: 5.5g Net

Fruity and Nutty Magical Donuts

Total time: 30 mins

Servings: 6

Ingredients:

½ cup erythritol

1/8 tsp baking soda

1 tsp stevia glycerite

1¼ cups almond milk

½ cup shredded coconut

¼ cup dry oranges

1/8 cup dried strawberries

¼ tsp coconut extract

2 cups blanched almond flour

1 tsp sea salt

1 tsp almond extract

3 large eggs3½ tsp baking powder

Directions:

Preheat the oven at 350 degrees and grease the donut pan with cooking spray.

Mix all the ingredients to make the donut batter and the pour the batter into the donut pan. Bake them in the preheated oven for 25 minutes and then allow complete cooling before serving.

Nutrition per Serving

Protein: 9g

Fat: 17g

Carbohydrate: 5.5g Net

Coconut Magic Donuts

Total time: 30 mins

Servings: 10

Ingredients:

    4 large eggs

    1 tsp baking powder

    ¼ tsp stevia

    ¼ cup erythritol

    ½ cup coconut flour

    ½ cup almond milk

    Coconut oil for frying

    ½ tsp vanilla

    ¼ cup melted coconut oil

    ¼ tsp salt

    ¼ cup lightly toasted shredded coconut (for topping)

    ¼ cup powdered erythritol (for topping)

Directions:

Mix the dry and wet ingredients in separate bowls and then blend them together to make the batter. Pour the batter in coated donut pan and bake them in preheated oven at 325 degrees for 16 minutes. Keep the donuts on wire rack for complete cooling.

Mix the shredded coconut and erythritol and keep the mixture in a bowl.

Heat oil in a pan and fry the donuts. They must be fried till they turn golden brown in color. Now dip the hot donuts into the coconut mixture and press slightly so that the topping sticks firmly.

Nutrition per Serving

Protein: 2g

Fat: 13g

Carbohydrate: 3g Net

Healthy and Tasty Pumpkin Blast

Total time: 15 mins

Servings: 5

Ingredients:

　　2 tbsp coconut flour

　　1 egg

　　½ tsp baking powder

　　¼ cup pumpkin puree

　　½ tsp pumpkin spice

　　1 packet of stevia

　　1 tbsp cocoa powder

　　2 tbsp almond milk

Directions:

Preheat the oven at 350 degrees and coat the donut pan with cooking spray.

Blend all the ingredients in a bowl to make smooth batter.

Pour the batter into the donut pan and bake them for 13 minutes. Cool them down by placing on wire rack and then serve.

Nutrition per Serving

Protein: 1g

Fat: 3g

Carbohydrate: 2.3g Net

Cheese Coated Chocolaty Donuts:

Total time: 30 mins

Servings: 10

Ingredients for making chocolaty donuts:

- 1 tsp xanthan gum
- ¼ cup granulated erythritol
- ½ tsp salt
- 2 tsp baking powder
- ¼ cup whey protein powder
- 3 tbsp cocoa powder
- ¼ cup butter
- 6 oz Greek yogurt
- ½ tsp baking soda
- 2 cups almond flour
- ¼ cup almond milk
- 15 drops red gel food color
- 10 drops stevia extract
- ½ tsp vanilla extract
- 3 eggs

Ingredients for making cheese coating:

2 tbsp butter

½ tsp stevia extract

8 drops of stevia extract

¼ cup powdered erythritol

4 oz cream cheese

¼ cup heavy cream

Directions:

Blend the yogurt and butter in a bowl and mix the vanilla, stevia and eggs to it.

Put the dry ingredients in a bowl and blend thoroughly. Add this mixture to the wet mixture and then add the food color at the end.

Pour the batter into the greased donut pan and bake them for 20 minutes.

When the donuts are being cooked make the cheesy coating. Make the coating by blending all the ingredients together.

Spread the coating over the donuts and allow some resting time and then serve the donuts.

Nutrition per Serving

Protein: 1.3g

Fat: 6g

Carbohydrate: 8.3g Net

Blueberry Delightful Donuts with orange Coating

Total time: 25 mins

Servings: 12

Ingredients for making blueberry donuts:

   1½ tsp baking powder

   ½ tsp nutmeg

   1 tsp xanthan gum

   ½ cup coconut flour

   ½ tsp salt

   1 cup almond flour

   ¼ cup frozen blueberries cooked in microwave oven for 30 seconds

   ½ cup almond milk

   ¼ tsp liquid stevia

   4 tbsp butter

   ½ cup powdered erythritol

   1 egg

Ingredients for making orange glaze:

   2 tbsp orange juice

1 tbsp frozen blueberries, cooked in microwave

¼ cup powdered erythritol

Few drops of orange flavouring

Directions:

Blend almond flour with coconut flour, baking powder, salt, nutmeg, xanthan gum and erythritol. Blend it by hand to make coarse crumbs.

Blend the blueberries with egg, stevia and almond milk and then add this mixture with the almond flour mixture. Make the batter smooth by using a hand blender.

Pour the batter into greased donut pan and bake them at 350 degrees for 12 minutes. Allow 10 minutes of cooling time.

Make the orange coating by mixing all the ingredients and then dip the donuts into the mixture. Allow some resting time so that the coating can set properly.

Nutrition per Serving

Protein: 3g

Fat: 10.1g

Carbohydrate: 2g Net

Simple Cream Glazed Donuts

Total time: 25 mins

Servings: 12

Ingredients for making donuts:

  2 cups almond flour

  ½ tsp slat

  2/3 cup cocoa powder

  ½ tsp baking soda

  1½ tsp baking powder

  1/3 cup granulated erythritol

  ¼ cup melted butter

  3 eggs, lightly beaten

  ½ cup almond milk

  ½ tsp xanthan gum

  20 drops of vanilla flavoured stevia

Ingredients for making cream glaze:

  3 tbsp Swedish cream liqueur

  3 tbsp almond milk

  ½ cup powdered erythritol

Directions:

Blend the dry and wet ingredients separately and then mix them together to make the donut batter. Pour the batter into oil coated pan and bake them for 20 minutes at 352 degrees. Allow complete cooling by keeping on wire rack.

Make the cheese glaze by mixing all the ingredients and spread this mixture over the donuts. Allow some resting time before serving.

Nutrition per Serving

Protein: 1.2g

Fat: 7g

Carbohydrate: 5g Net

Healthy and Spicy Spinach Donuts

Total time: 15 mins

Servings: 4

Ingredients:

½ tsp baking powder

1 cup spinach puree (homemade)

1 packet of stevia

2 egg whites

1/8 tsp cardamom powder

A pinch of cinnamon

2 tbsp coconut flour

A pinch of salt

Directions:

Blend all the ingredients to make smooth batter.

Pour the batter into greased donut pan and bake them for 15 minutes at 350 degrees. Allow complete cooling before serving.

Nutrition per Serving

Protein: 1.6g

Fat: 2.5g

Carbohydrate: 10.2g Net

Easy to make Strawberry Donuts

Total time: 15 mins

Servings: 4

Ingredients:

½ cup mashed strawberries

½ tsp baking powder

2 tbsp coconut flour

A pinch of cinnamon

A pinch of salt

1 packet of stevia

2 egg whites

Directions:

Blend all the ingredients to make smooth batter.

Pour the batter into donut pan and bake them at 350 degrees for 15 minutes. Allow complete cooling and then serve.

Nutrition per Serving

Protein: 1.6g

Fat: 2.5g

Carbohydrate: 10.2g Net

Double Orange Blast Donuts

Total time: 1 hr 20 mins

Servings: 12

Ingredients for making orange donuts:

   1 tbsp baking powder

   1 tbsp cinnamon

   3 cups almond flour

   4 eggs

   ½ cup butter

   2 cups swerve

   2 tsp orange extract

   1 tsp sea salt

   ¼ tsp nutmeg

   ½ cup orange juice

Ingredients for making orange glaze:

   ½ cup coconut oil

   ½ cup powdered erythritol

   1 tsp orange extract

Directions:

Mix the dry and wet ingredients separately and then blend them together to make smooth batter.

Pour the batter into greased donut pan and bake them for an hour at 350 degrees. Allow complete cooling after baking.

Make the orange glaze by mixing all the ingredients and coat the donuts with it. Serve after allowing some resting time.

Nutrition per Serving

Protein: 5g

Fat: 22g

Carbohydrate: 6.7g Net

Almond Punch Donuts

Total time: 1 hr 20 mins

Servings: 12

Ingredients for making almond flavored donuts:

   1 tbsp baking powder

   1 tbsp cinnamon

   3 cups almond flour

   4 eggs

   ½ cup butter

   2 cups swerve

   2 tsp almond extract

   1 tsp sea salt

   ¼ tsp nutmeg

Ingredients for making orange glaze:

   ½ cup coconut oil

   ½ cup powdered erythritol

   1 tsp almond extract

   Finely chopped almonds (for final topping)

Directions:

Blend the dry and wet ingredients separately and then mix them to make smooth batter.

Pour the batter into greased donut pan and bake at 350 degrees for an hour. Allow complete cooling by placing the donuts on wire rack.

Make the almond glaze by mixing the ingredients and keep the chopped almonds aside.

Spread the glaze mixture over the donuts and sprinkle the chopped almonds on top and allow enough time so that the topping can set.

Nutrition per Serving

Protein: 5g

Fat: 22g

Carbohydrate: 6.7g Net

Choco-Nutty Fantastic Donut

Total time: 16 mins

Servings: 8

Ingredients for making donuts:

　3 eggs

　¼ tsp baking soda

　1/3 cup cocoa powder

　A pinch of sea salt

　1/3 cup powdered erythritol

　¼ cup butter

　1/8 tsp almond flavoring

　¾ cup packed almond flour

　½ tsp apple cider vinegar

Ingredients for making chocolate coating:

　2 tbsp butter

　1 oz unsweetened chocolate

　3 tbsp powdered erythritol

　Finely chopped almonds for final topping

Directions:

Blend the dry and wet ingredients separately and then mix them together to make smooth batter.

Pour the batter into the greased donut pan and bake them at 350 degrees for 15 minutes. While the donuts are being baked you will have to make the chocolate glaze by melting the chocolate in microwave oven and then mix the other ingredients. Make sure to keep the chopped almonds aside. Coat the donuts with the chocolate glaze and then sprinkle the chopped almonds on to. Allow some resting time before serving.

Nutrition per Serving

Protein: 3.2g

Fat: 6.9g

Carbohydrate: 2.1g Net

Vanilla and Chocolate Smashing Donuts

Total time: 16 mins

Servings: 8

Ingredients for making chocolate donuts:

　A pinch of sea salt

　¾ cup packed almond flour

　¼ cup butter

　3 eggs

　1/3 cup powdered erythritol

　1/3 cup cocoa powder

　1/8 tsp chocolate flavoring

　½ tsp apple cider vinegar

　¼ tsp baking soda

Ingredients for making vanilla coating:

　1 oz unsweetened heavy cream

　3 tbsp powdered erythritol

　2 tbsp butter

　¼ tsp vanilla flavor

Directions:

Blend the wet and dry ingredients separately and then mix them together to make smooth batter.

Pour the batter into greased donut pan and bake them at 350 degrees for 15 minutes. Allow complete cooling after baking.

Make the vanilla coating mixture by mixing all the ingredients. Spread the coating mixture on the donuts and allow some resting time before serving.

Nutrition per Serving

Protein: 3.2g

Fat: 6.9g

Carbohydrate: 2.1g Net

Simplest Chocolate Donuts

Total time: 15 mins

Servings: 12

Ingredients:

¾ cup erythritol

½ tsp vanilla extract

4 oz unsweetened chocolate

¼ cup cocoa powder

12 tbsp butter

5 eggs

Directions:

Melt the butter and then blend all the ingredients with it to make the donut batter. Pour the batter into greased donut pan.

Bake them at 325 degrees for 15 minutes and allow a bit of resting before serving.

Nutrition per Serving

Protein: 4.8g

Fat: 6g

Carbohydrate: 3.8g Net

Mom's Magic Strawberry Donuts

Total time: 15 mins

Servings: 12

Ingredients:

¼ cup cocoa powder

¾ cup erythritol

1/8 tsp strawberry flavoring

12 tbsp butter, melted

¼ cup mashed strawberries

5 eggs

4 oz unsweetened chocolate

Directions:

Blend all the ingredients to make smooth batter. Using a hand blender will make the work easy.

Grease the donut pan with cooking spray and bake the donuts at 325 degrees for 15 minutes. Allow cooling before serving.

Nutrition per Serving

Protein: 4.8g

Fat: 6g

Carbohydrate: 3.8g Net

Banana & Coconut Protein Punch

Total time: 15 mins

Servings: 12

Ingredients:

1 mashed banana

¼ cup shredded coconut

1/3 liquid egg white

2 tbsp coconut flour

1 tsp baking soda

2 tsp liquid stevia

2 tbsp almond milk

1 tbsp powdered erythritol

4 tbsp protein powder

½ tsp ground cinnamon

Directions:

Blend the wet and dry ingredients in separate bowls and then mix them together to make smooth batter.

Pour the batter into greased donut pan and bake them in the preheated oven for 15 minutes at 350 degrees. Allow cooling before serving.

Nutrition per Serving

Protein: 2g

Fat: 0.6g

Carbohydrate: 1.7g Net

Protein Boosting Strawberry Donuts

Total time: 15 mins

Servings: 12

Ingredients:

   1 cup mashed strawberries

   1/3 liquid egg white

   2 tbsp coconut flour

   1 tsp baking soda

   2 tsp liquid stevia

   2 tbsp almond milk

   1 tbsp powdered erythritol

   4 tbsp protein powder

   ½ tsp ground cinnamon

Directions:

Blend the wet and dry ingredients separately and then mix them together to make smooth batter. It will be best to use an immersion blender for this task.

Grease the donut pan with cooking spray and pour the batter into it.

Bake the donuts at 350 degrees for 15 minutes and then allow cooling on wire rack.

Nutrition per Serving

Protein: 2g

Fat: 0.6g

Carbohydrate: 1.7g Net

Pumpkin Pie Flavorful Donuts

Total time: 30 mins

Servings: 6

Ingredients:

　1 cup almond flour

　½ tsp cinnamon

　2 eggs

　¼ tsp sea salt

　½ tsp baking soda

　1/3 cup erythritol

　½ cup chopped walnuts

　¾ cup pumpkin (grated)

　1 tbsp butter

　¼ tsp pumpkin spice

　¼ cup unsweetened cocoa powder

　1 tbsp almond milk

Directions:

Blend the wet and dry ingredients in separate bowls and then mix them together to make smooth batter. It will be best to use a hand blender.

Pour the batter into greased donut pan and then bake them for 30 minutes at 350 degrees. Serve after cooling the donuts on wire rack.

Nutrition per Serving

Protein: 9.2g

Fat: 19.3g

Carbohydrate: 7.7g Net

Magical Spicy Zucchini Donuts

Total time: 30 mins

Servings: 12

Ingredients:

1 cup almond flour

½ tsp cinnamon

2 eggs

¼ tsp sea salt

½ tsp baking soda

1/3 cup erythritol

½ cup chopped walnuts

¾ cup grated zucchini

1 tbsp butter

¼ cup unsweetened cocoa powder

1 tbsp almond milk

Directions:

Blend the wet and dry ingredients separately and then mix them together using a hand blender to make smooth batter.

Pour the batter in donut pan and bake at 350 degrees for 30 minutes.

Allow cooling and then serve.

Nutrition per Serving

Protein: 9.2g

Fat: 19.3g

Carbohydrate: 7.7g Net

Apple-Maple Mysterious Donut

Total time: 15 mins

Servings: 12

Ingredients:

  1 apple, mashed

  1 tsp maple syrup

  1/3 liquid egg white

  2 tbsp coconut flour

  4 tbsp protein powder

  ½ tsp ground cinnamon

  1 tsp baking soda

  2 tsp liquid stevia

  2 tbsp almond milk

  1 tbsp powdered erythritol

Directions:

Blend all the ingredients together in food processor to make smooth batter for donuts.

Grease the donut pan with cooking spray and pour the batter into it. Bake them at 350 degrees for 15 minutes and then put on wire rack for cooling.

Nutrition per Serving

Protein: 2g

Fat: 0.6g

Carbohydrate: 1.7g Net

Raspberry Sweet Fantasy Donut

Total time: 15 mins

Servings: 12

Ingredients:

   1 cup mashed raspberries

   1/3 liquid egg white

   ¼ cup raspberry syrup

   2 tbsp coconut flour

   4 tbsp protein powder

   ½ tsp ground cinnamon

   1 tsp baking soda

   2 tsp liquid stevia

   2 tbsp almond milk

   2 tbsp powdered erythritol

Directions:

Mix the wet and dry ingredients in separate bowls and then blend the two mixtures to make the donut batter.

Pour the batter into the donut pan and bake them at 350 degrees for 15 minutes. Serve after cooling.

Nutrition per Serving

Protein: 2g

Fat: 0.6g

Carbohydrate: 1.7g Net

Nut Blast Donuts with Cheese Topping

Total time: 30 mins

Servings: 12

Ingredients for making donuts:

1 cup almond flour

¼ cup chopped almonds

¼ cup peanut butter

2 eggs

¼ cup powdered erythritol

1/8 cup chopped pecans

¼ tsp vanilla flavor

¼ tsp cinnamon powder

Ingredients for making cheese topping:

½ cup cheese

¼ cup butter

1/8 cup powdered erythritol

Directions:

Blend the wet and dry ingredients and then mix them together to make the donut batter. The batter will be full of nuts and thus not smooth.

Pour the batter into the greased donut pan and bake them at 350 degrees for 30 minutes.

When the donuts are being cooked, add the ingredients to make the cheese topping. Spread the cheese coating over the donuts and allow some resting time so that the coating can set.

Nutrition per Serving

Protein: 3g

Fat: 1.6g

Carbohydrate: 1.2g Net

Made in the USA
Middletown, DE
06 April 2018